Unlawful Sex and other Testy Matters

Unlawful Sex and other Testy Matters

by

JOHN B. KEANE

THE MERCIER PRESS

CORK

THE MERCIER PRESS,
Cork

© John B. Keane, 1978

ISBN 978 1 78117 899 7

TO JOANNA

Transferred to Digital Print-on-Demand in 2024

CONTENTS

Unlawful Sex	7
Things that happen in Bed	13
Calls of Nature	19
Primroses	26
The Hatbox Incident	30
Unusual Catches	34
Breaking Wind	38
Young Love	44
The Lost Art of Capping Eggs	50
August Thoughts	56
Big Words	63
Bed Hermits	67
Skillet Pots	71
Canavan's Dog	76
The Lost Heifer	80
Food Dressings	85
Mixed Grills	89

UNLAWFUL SEX

Illicit sex is bad for the heart. I do not say so personally but it is now widely believed in continental medical circles that sex without a license will put paid to the beating of the most consistent ticker. It was also accepted in a limited way by certain of the religious who, fair play to them, insisted for starters that it was bad for marriage first and for a number of other things afterwards.

I remember a fiery missioner with whom I often imbibed a few whiskies when he would finish up for the evening. During one of his sermons he described a married man who had left his wife's couch for the couch of another.

'This heinous wretch,' said he, 'was not content with going to hell himself, oh no he had to take another unfortunate soul with him.'

One night, however, it transpired that after a night with his mistress the fellow was seized by an inexplicable pain in the forehead. He fell to the ground never to rise again. According to the missioner if he had loved his own woman instead of fornicating with another he would still be in the land of the living.

That night I asked him if the story was true. He

swallowed a drop of his whiskey and looked me squarely between the eyes.

'Who's to say?' he said. 'Anyway,' he went on, 'twasn't to tell 'em fairy stories the parish priest brought me all this way. I will tell you this, however,' and he paused to finish his glass, 'a man without the grace of God has no peace of mind and a man with no peace of mind cannot possibly lead a normal life. A man who does not lead a normal life cannot expect to live a long life. Therefore, a man who indulges in unlawful sex should be prepared for a premature departure from the land of the living.'

I remember at the time I found my friend's logic acceptable. In fact I still do. More recently I read in a Sunday newspaper where Professor Bernhard Krauland of the University of West Berlin was quoted as saying that 'extra-marital sex is bad for the hearts of middle-aged men.'

According to Krauland lovemaking in the marital bed is a healthy exercise whereas the middle-aged man who goes to bed with his secretary could be flirting with death.

I wasn't all that interested in the good Professor's claims for the simple reason that here was another gambit or exercise which was bad for the heart. Almost everything these days from beer to butter and bad thoughts to Bingo is blamed for the high incidence of heart disease. There is no day now that some newspaper doesn't carry an account of new cardiac dangers arising from the consumption of too many overfried sausages or tying one's laces too tight.

I must say, however, that I found the Professor's revelations intriguing so on the Wednesday after reading the newspapers I took myself to the bog of Dirha West. Sonny Canavan was alive and well at the time. How we have all grown to miss that seer, sage and sensible man.

I found him counting his goats near an ass passage. Over our heads curlews wheeled and bleated in the rain-filled skies. The goats grazed happily and one might say that the scene was a truly pastoral one. Background music of a high quality was supplied by a concealed roadside brook. Having concluded his goat-count Canavan turned his nose directly into the wind. He did not sniff. Rather did he scent the air.

'Rain,' he announced, 'heavy and long without a break.'

We walked along the narrow roadway picking our steps between the clusters of shining marbles, freshly deposited by the constipation-free goats.

As we savoured the salt-laden, southwesterly wind I conveyed Professor Krauland's findings to Canavan.

'What's he a professor of?' was Canavan's first question.

'Medicine,' I replied.

'With regard to sleeping with secretaries,' said

Canavan, 'he may be right and he may be wrong. Who am I to disagree with him that never had a clerk not to mind a secretary.'

Once more I quoted from Professor Krauland.

'According to this man,' I said, 'a girlfriend is usually more demanding than a wife.'

'That,' said Canavan,' 'would depend on the wife.'

'Are you saying the Professor is wrong?'

'What I'm saying is this,' said Canavan and a frown appeared on his unshaven face, 'a bird in the hand is worth two in the bush. A wife in the bed is worth two outside of it. The wife is where the action is. The others are not.'

Again I quoted from Professor Krauland: 'Most of the lovers who die in their girlfriend's beds are between fifty and fifty-nine.'

Canavan paused. 'There's a man we both know,' said Canavan, 'lives not far from here. He has three wives planted in a graveyard that you often wrote about. Single, married or widowed he ramboozled all makes of women as fast as you'd pull 'em out from under him. 'Twas the nature of the poor man. Some men are wild for drink, some for money and more for travel but there's others, like our man, and sex comes as natural to them as it does to the puck or the pony stallion.'

'That man,' said Canavan, 'is past a hundred years of age. He has an appetite like a horse for fresh mate or salty. He has the health of a spring salmon and the same desire for women that he had eighty years ago.'

We walked towards the main road which links Listowel and Ballybunion. Canavan looked at the heavens. His nose twitched, a sure sign of rain. The skies darkened and in the distance beyond the fabled hills of Cnocanore there was the faintest rumble of thunder. From above us there came a long, confidential whisper and suddenly a vast flock of starlings whirred by over our heads. A fat, shawled woman, a legacy from our far off yesterdays, rode by in an ass-cart.

'Good morrow men,' she called but flicked her reins rather than tax herself with heeding our replies. She had sufficient on her mind. The ass trotted off briskly at the wrong side of the road. Canavan stopped and tapped me gently on the chest with his index finger.

'Most of those,' said he, 'that tended their wives and their wives alone are presently growing daisies while your man that lifted every skirt in sight is still hale and hearty and there's no one knows him will deny that he gave more time in the beds of others than he gave in his own. The man was a born ramboozler. It came as natural to him as crowing to a cock or braying to a donkey. If this doctor is right the man should be dead fifty years ago whereas he's still alive and kicking as any respectable female around these parts will verify.'

'But,' said I, 'Professor Krauland maintains that sex outside marriage is bad for the heart because it's so much more exciting than lawful sex.'

'Of course it's exciting,' Canavan said, 'only a fool

would say otherwise and I'll grant you while it might be bad for some hearts it's just the job for more hearts. There's no two hearts alike no more than there's two doctors' opinions alike.'

'One more question,' I said.

'Fire away,' said Canavan.

'Professor Krauland says that extra-marital sex carries hidden dangers. What have you to say to that?'

'Plum pudding carries hidden dangers,' Canavan replied. 'So does fried bread and so does bottled stout, even gettin' out of bed does whether there's a secretary in it or not.'

So saying he turned and faced for his house after raising a hand in silent farewell. The Oracle of Dirha had spoken.

THINGS THAT HAPPEN IN BED

There are millions of songs about sex, love and romance, not necessarily in that order, whereas there are hardly any songs at all about that area where ninety per cent of the lovemaking of the civilised world takes place. There are five hundred evergreen ballads about tropical beaches for every one about a bed. Ninety-nine per cent of us are the product of that most widely-used of all love-couches commonly referred to as the double-bed and yet we are strangely remiss in our appreciation of it. For every one of us conceived in haysheds, motorcars, river banks, alleyways, meadows, pastures, lakesides and uninhabited islands there are ninety-nine of us conceived in bed, be that bed double or single. The only song I learned, as a youth, to have anything to do with beds was the *Three Lovely Lasses* and this was only a passing reference:

> My mother has forty fine shillings, shillings, shillings.
> My mother has forty fine shillings
> And she'll leave me her bed when she dies.

Of course in those days beds were mostly made of iron and could withstand all sorts of abuse whereas nowadays beds are designed for comfort rather than endurance. You ask any hotelier or guesthouse-keeper and they will tell you that weak beds make no battle with honeymoon couples whereas with older people beds have a far longer lifetime. Also beds made from lightweight materials soon turn rickety and are only fit for sleeping in. This is why it is so important to get a good bed when you marry. It should be a bed for all seasons if you follow, not just for the halcyon honeymoon days nor for the maturing years but one for the full round of a lifetime, a bed, in short, capable of coping with the whims, storms and flurries of a pair who have contracted to weather out the remainder of life's years together. You need a most reliable barque for such a long and comprehensive voyage so that the best available in good double-beds is a sound investment and one which will pay juicy dividends on wet nights and dry, humid and frosty, windy and calm. Young married people expect too much from their beds whereas those who possess normal expectations can be assured of bright bedtimes.

Few people fail to realise, until it is too late, that family histories have been written in bed and if double-beds could talk they would a tale unfold to make *Gone with the Wind* read like a bedtime story. To me there is no sight so sad as an empty, second-hand, double-bed with a 'For Sale' sign tagged to one of its extremities as it stands sundered and exposed against the wall of a colourless auction room. The more worn and decrepit the bed the more interesting the story it has to tell. It is indeed an unfitting end for a vehicle which so often transported its loving occupants on journeys of exalted bliss. Every double-bed has its own tale to tell. Of this you may be certain and a wide audience awaits the author who puts his name beneath the title 'The Life and Times of a Double-Bed'. Here surely is a natural best-seller if ever there was one.

The double-bed is the last refuge of the fractured marriage, the sole haven of nightmare-stricken children, the only place on this earth where silence wins every battle in the finish and the proper place to end all wars until the next one. It is the hatchery of every family plot, the blueprint board for designing the futures of every offspring and a good place to hide under if you are a man who shuns violence. It is a place to retire to when debts mount and survival seems impossible. There is no better sanctum to weather out bad publicity and if you are a man who has fallen foul of the law, who needs time and rest to gather wits and muster courage the bed is your man while your solicitor is applying for an adjournment.

The first bed we bought was a sooner, that is to say a bed which would sooner squeak than induce sleep. It would sooner be croaking and groaning all night than fulfilling its true role of consoler and comforter. I once leaped from it in despair thinking I would never sleep again. In the process I badly barked my astragalus and was confined to it for several days. At the slightest movement of either of our bodies it protested in the most irritating way possible. It never stopped. You couldn't breathe without a responding squeak. Neighbours could hear it quite plainly and one made so bold as to ask sarcastically if our honeymoon would ever end. Still and for all it served its purpose for noisome and ill-made as it was it indentured us partly in the mastery of double-beds. It taught us that young married couples starting out in life should never be trusted with a new double-bed no more than apprentice drivers should be presented with new motor-cars.

We sold this bed to a relation of mine who was ever on the alert for bargains. It didn't matter whether he wanted the bed or not. So long as it was well under the market price he couldn't resist no matter what the object for sale was. He now keeps it in his spare room and invites visiting couples to spend a night in it. Those that do lie absolutely still since the slightest movement is advertised by squeaks and protestations which can be heard in the farthest corners of the house.

Our next bed was a firmer, stouter, stronger couch and it was given to occasional, long-drawn-out groans rather than endless squeaking. It was comfortable too and it hadn't cost us much. Then one night I turned over on it and it collapsed. The missus thought we were being assassinated and all my protestations did not succeed in stifling the chilling scream which rose from her throat at the instant of collapse. Now the neighbours would really have something to talk about. The very least, they would say she got, was a broken nose. We repaired the bed quickly and in no time at all we were sleeping like two tops. The next bed we bought was an expensive, shapely affair with a six-months guarantee. It broke up like a floundering ship when I collapsed on to it one night after a wedding. I slept away oblivious of the fact that I was on the floor. The guarantee was honoured and we got another one of identical shape and size. Then one night a week afterwards I jumped out of bed to fling a tin of talcum powder at a howling canine who was disrupting my sleep. It was when I leapt back that the bed fell apart. The missus woke and made only one comment before removing herself to the spare.

'Some night you'll kill me,' she said.

The next bed we bought we still have and it is my considered opinion that it will be our last investment in this type of article. It can withstand any assault. Seldom or ever does it make a noise and then only under severe provocation. Its most valuable single asset is that nobody but its occupants ever know what goes on in it and this is the *sine qua non* of your worthwhile bed. This bed is wide and deep and its only fault is that one tends to oversleep in it. On the credit side it is a bed which throws people out who do not belong in it and whenever the missus and I are away should one of the offspring decide to sleep in it he will find himself on the floor before morning.

Contrary to widespread belief oversized people are no danger to the life of a bed. Neither are fat people nor those who posses both ingredients, i.e., bigness and fatness. No. Your thin, wiry individual whether male or female is the liveliest and most restless in bed. The big and the fat move rarely and when they do their movements are ponderous and predictable. Not so with your lightweight. He is forever twisting and turning and jumping up and down and kicking the clothes off. This man is better off sleeping on the floor. Imagine, therefore, what effect two of the same ilk would have on your ordinary bed. Surely the bed is doomed from the beginning.

The missus wants me to buy a new bed once more. She brings up the subject from time to time. I'll keep putting her off because I'm just getting used to the one I have and it's just getting used to me after a confrontation which has lasted most of my married life.

There are people reading this who may be tempted to ask if this treatise is worth all the trouble. They may say a bed is just a bed, an inanimate body of springs, timber, stuffing and cloth. But I say look to your bed as you would to your house, for you will spend one-third of your lifetime lying down and unless you're a donkey you'll do your lying down in a bed.

CALLS OF NATURE

When I was a gorsoon there were no toilet rolls in our house.

The same applied to every house in the street. There were, of course, many alternatives. The most common was your accurately divided newspaper or magazine, cut carefully into rectangular pieces consisting of an approximate area of thirty square inches. These would be neatly sheafed together and the top left hand corner would be perforated with an awl.

Through the perforation a slender cord was thrust until equal parts of this cord extended from each side of the sheaf. Both ends were then knotted together and the whole hung from a nail in that place referred to as the privy or closet.

In country dwellings where there were no such edifices, the countryside itself, meaning its more privately appointed groves and dells, was used for calls of nature.

Logically, one could not expect to find sheaves of paper hanging from the bushes and trees in these isolated places. Mankind, however, always inventive and ingenious in awkward circumstances, turned to the leaves of the trees for a fully comprehensive toilet service.

Where leaves were not available there was other

greenery, satin-textured and otherwise, for those of different tastes.

The most commonly used plant was the dock and your ordinary dock leaf was without peer in this most private and embarrassing of functions. Any stout-stemmed plant with broad leaves substituted admirably. Then you had an abundance of lichens, mosses and other tender cryptogamic plants without peer in this field.

Indeed we have mention in history books of Queens and Empresses being favourably disposed towards the softer members of the moss family.

Purely for the record's sake, let me say that in China long before Chairman Mao's ascendancy the emperors and nobles of that vast country were in the habit of using goslings and ducklings for this chore. After each exercise the creatures were released, unlike hare coursing where the victims are used again and again regardless of their feelings in the matter.

Let us return, however, to our friend the countryman and extend the theme of toilet materials a little further if for no other purpose than to enlighten today's pampered public in the event of their being caught short as it were in places far removed from fully equipped public and private lavatories.

Your countryman in the absence of mosses, lichens and dock leaves, could always turn to mother earth herself and her fleecy cloak of rich green grasses. Those unfortunate enough to be the possessors of tender or inflamed or indeed hyper-sensitive posteriors sought other than grass for the removal of impurities, defilements and what-have-you.

These unfortunates would betake themselves to the vicinity of a small stream or river and upon finishing the business in hand might sit themselves down in a shallow but fast-flowing stream. There, happily, they might sit and ponder while the cleansing waters did the dirty work, so to speak.

In these blissful surroundings such afflicted souls might listen to the soft music of murmuring waters or hearken to the delightful melodies of the innumerable birds which people the trees and bushes standing along the banks of these beneficial waterways.

There is the danger, however, that these absent-minded recumbents might submit more than their posteriors to the laving waters for it is a known fact that unexpected floods have often carried off the unsuspecting and the drowsy without as much as a tweet of apology and with no regard for the feelings of those left behind.

Such is nature, gentle and advantageous one minute and the next, savage and remorseless.

These unexpected disasters should serve to remind us that although it is the most commonplace of human functions it should never be embarked upon without careful investigation of the immediate lie of the land. Otherwise tragedy and misfortune may raise their ugly heads.

In the absence of an indoor toilet those seeking

outdoor relief would be well advised to check the ground beneath their feet and to examine the texture of the foliage and grasses in their immediate vicinities. The approaches should also be taken account for in the great outdoors you never know from whence danger is likely to threaten.

A small scenic glade is the most admirable of all retreats in this respect. The drowsy buzzing of bees and the whisper of gentle winds in the overhead foliage have much the same effect as a muted background orchestra although there are many who prefer to read a book or magazine while so preoccupied.

It is vital to locate a place well removed from the alarums and bustle of the world.

It is often wise to follow cowpaths for these end under shady bowers in the quiet corners of green fields or they lead to serene, secluded, out-of-the-way places beneath lofty river banks. Your only danger here is from frolicsome bull calves who will simulate the stance and rage of their elders and indeed often chance an assault if they think they can get away with it.

Some readers may find it surprising in this day and age to find people who cannot avail themselves of indoor toilets. These unfortunates suffer mostly from nervous disorders or claustraphobia and there are also a few, an adventurous few, who risk the outdoors purely for the sake of adventure.

In Listowel up until a few short years ago there was a man who used to climb trees in order to relieve himself. God help an unwary passer-by and a thousand woes to him who upon hearing a rustle overhead felt obliged to gaze upwards.

Anthropologists would do well to study men of this ilk. It might prove conclusively that man is indeed descended from the great apes and that now and then much of this apishness surfaces unbidden. It might account also for much of the horse-play, vandalism and violence so prevalent at the present time.

To return to our Listowel friend, it must be said in fairity to the man that he chose only remote arboreal retreats. His preference for the outdoors ended on a January evening when the bough upon which he was perched was assailed by an unexpected gale of wind. Already the bough was slippery from the rains of the previous night.

Our unfortunate friend was more or less in what we may call a 'lavatory trance' when the calamity occurred. In vain did he try to maintain his balance, but the odds, alas, were stacked against him. He was caught, as the saying goes, with his trousers down.

With a fearful shriek he fell to the ground, breaking upon landing his collarbone, some odd ribs and his left leg. He would not climb a tree now for love or money nor indeed for any other reason no matter how pressing.

There was another individual, an acquaintance of mine now happily married in Canada, who refused all indoor amenities on the grounds that they tended to soften the human race and make them too dependant on gadgets and aids.

The individual favoured the tops of cliffs — seaside, land-locked and riverside — and let it be forever to the credit of his innate acrobatic endowments that he never once came a cropper.

Townspeople who may have originally come from a countryside where such outdoor practices were condoned and tolerated have become softened by indoor life and by the availability of bathrooms or water closets. A sight which once might have provoked no more than a sly smile now causes outrage and fears are expressed for the safety of innocent children as well as women.

Country people are more aware of the vagaries of inconsistent bladders. They know what it is to be 'stuck' so to speak and their sympathies are wholeheartedly on the side of the man who is unable to retain his impurities.

At this juncture the reader will be sure to ask why the victim did not avail himself of a public toilet especially since most towns boast fine examples of these. Easier said than done. There are many country people who will not entrust themselves to the interior of a public toilet for love or money. One might be locked in and allowed to languish for days, even forever. A public toilet is like a prison in some respects. It is also impersonal and who knows what might befall an innocent countryman were he to risk a visit there.

No. Better to risk prosecution by availing oneself

of a by-way, an archway or the side of a convenient and empty motor car. This way a man is dependant on nobody but himself and may retain the link with the great outdoors where his heart really belongs.

PRIMROSES

I love primroses, loveliest of perennials, set in cosy cushions of curdled green. They do not need me to extol them for they are the brightest gems of spring and have been truly loved and cherished by balladmakers and poets since man first began to make rhythm from velvety vowels and clearcut consonants.

Therefore, I will not sing of primroses as such but rather of places where these heartening sprays abide as against other unfortunate spots where they never take root.

The primrose is to be found mostly at the shady side of ditches and knolls, the bases of strong trees and in the lee of walls tall and small, in short, where frost is prohibited and breezes bereft of space to blow as boldly as they'd like.

I have also unexpectedly come across them in the lanes and by-ways of towns and cities. These urban bohareens offer shade and shelter to the peerless primrose.

The primrose, although closely related to water violets, cyclamens and pimpernels, lives apart, though not aloofly, from all other flowers, saving the gentle violet whose company is obviously acceptable, for I have seen them sharing the same bed in high compliment to each other.

Your primrose, however, is a strange and mysterious visitor in many ways. It will grow only where it chooses as I know to my cost. I remember I once transferred several sizeable clumps complete with parent clay from a hedge near Ballybunion to a hedge near Listowel. Alas, they failed and died and I regret the experiment now.

However, I transferred another clump from the base of a protective chestnut tree to the corner of my father's grave where they took root at once.

The simple truth of the matter is that there are roads for primroses just as surely as there are horses for courses and it is a shame that these chosen areas have never been charted and presented to a primrose hungry public by some astute firm of cartographers.

The road between Ballybunion and Listowel is a well known habitat of primroses but they refuse to appear at the built up extremities of both towns for reasons which no one can explain.

The road between Limerick and Nenagh is a disaster area for primroses but not so the road between Nenagh and Roscrea, for all along this busy highway there are countless clusters of these eye-catching charmers.

The road from Athlone to Roscommon as I recall, is another well known primrose sanctuary, particularly before and after the village of Knockcroghery which places, for some inexplicable reason, play host to more primroses than you'd find in the entire road between Galway and Limerick.

The narrower roads of Mayo are also highly popular with primroses and there are certain hedges on the way to Claremorris which are literally coloured yellow such is the inexplicable primrose prosilience in these otherwise depopulated places.

Lucky indeed are the men and women who live in primrose country because when clouds are dun-coloured or slate-grey with impending rain they will light the scene as no other flowers can and lift the drooping heart to extraordinary heights.

It is odd, therefore, that so many of the songs which carry mention of primroses should be so full of melancholy. Shakespeare too warns us about treading 'the primrose path of dalliance' when he might easily have chosen the common dogrose or piss-a-bed. Why bring the pride and joy of spring into life's sorry and everlasting argument.

I remember, too, many years ago to be drinking porter in Mikey Joe O'Connor's back lounge in Ballybunion. It was a wet Sunday in August and only ducks were out of doors. Suddenly a busload of women from the city of Limerick entered the lounge and in no time at all a spirited singsong was in full swing. The highlight of the afternoon was supposed to be a moustachioed melodeon player who was attached to the premises.

He sang through his nose while his voice was filled with emotion. When he came to the saddest verse there was an intense hush and the scoundrel knew he had his audience by the heart-strings.

> There were snowdrops and primroses
> Piled high around her bed
> And Ferns Church was crowded
> When her funeral Mass was said

I looked about me out of curiosity and saw that there wasn't a dry eye in the room. In protest I got up and walked out without finishing my glass of stout because I believe that primroses should not be associated with grief.

They are constant and true and they brave the bitterness of winter to remind us that spring is at hand and the cuckoo thinking of booking his passage from distant Africa.

THE HATBOX INCIDENT

One man's food is another man's poison or to put it another way beauty is often in the eye of the beholder. The following story is a true one and has to do with the aforementioned cliches. Every story should have a name. I, therefore, christen this tale 'The Hatbox Incident'.

More accomplished storytellers might not be so prosaic. Even so I stick to my title.

The year 1947 was a great year for lobsters. The summer had been an outstanding one and in those days the number of boats fishing for this prized catch was a mere fraction of what it is today. The species was bigger and more succulent and you could buy the cream of any catch for a pittance. In north Kerry the number of people who had eaten lobster could be counted on the fingers of two hands.

The coast north of the Feale has never been a favourite haunt of these highly edible crustaceans. Consequently most of the people of that district, particularly inland, had never even seen not to mention having consumed a lobster.

It was a Sunday afternoon. The town of Listowel was peaceful and quiet. Most of its population had been transported one way or another to the seaside resort of Ballybunion which is only nine miles distant. Market Street was the only one of the town's thoroughfares which showed any degree of life.

Now and then an ass-rail of turf trundled by on its way to a shed for winter storage. One of these transports having discharged its load was about to move off in the direction of Dirha Bog for another cargo when a large motor-car suddenly drew up alongside.

Its driver informed the donkey's driver that he had been endeavouring for several minutes to gain access to a certain premises not too far away. Despite repeated knocking there was no response whatsoever.

'Ah, they would be in Ballybunion,' said the driver whose name was Charlie. 'I seen them and they goin' there early in the day.'

'That's a pity since I have a message here for them,' said the car driver.

'I'll tell you what,' said Charlie, 'why don't you leave the message inside with my missus and when your friends return from Ballybunion I'll deliver it for you.'

So saying Charlie addressed himself to his ass and they moved off. The car driver took a large hatbox from the boot of the car and handed it to Charlie's missus, whose name happened to be Maggie.

She deposited the box in a corner of the kitchen and returned to the table where she had been engaged with the making of a few mutton hand grenades, i.e. meatballs for Charlie's supper.

Diligently she applied herself to her work, humming a snatch of an ancient melody as she kneaded the constituents of the meatballs.

Then inexplicably the cover of the hatbox rose and fell. Maggie clutched her breast and crossed herself fervently hoping that she had been mistaken. But no, the cover rose and fell a second time. She ran to the doorway and lifted the holy water font from the nail which secured it to the wall.

She flung its contents at the hatbox and screamed when a glistening black claw appeared suddenly at the box's rim. This was surely the devil about which the missioners had often warned herself and others during times of Retreat

The first claw was followed by a second and then by several spidery antennae each one more hideous than the next. Never before had she beheld anything so horrifying. She could hardly believe her eyes.

Maggie screamed again, again and again. Luckily Charlie was just returning with another load of turf. He rushed into the kitchen where he beheld the monster which had just emerged, in toto, from the hatbox. He stood rooted to the ground as another monster of similar shape followed the first.

'What in God's name will we do?' Maggie screamed.

'I don't know about you,' Charlie cried out, 'but I'm goin' to attack.'

With that he seized the iron tongs from the fireplace while Maggie laid hold of the sweeping brush. Without further ado and with frightful imprecations the pair laid into the luckless lobsters.

A battle royal raged for several minutes but the creatures from the hatbox were no match for the enraged humans. They were beaten and kicked out the back door which Charlie had the foresight to open as soon as he scented victory.

Later that evening when Maggie opened the back door to eject the kitchen sweepings there was no sign of the vanquished. The local dog population had lobster for supper that evening.

So ended 'The Hatbox Incident'. Never before I'm sure did a brace of prime lobsters end their days in such a fashion.

UNUSUAL CATCHES

During my first serious day's fishing with rod and line I hooked and landed a size four lady's shoe. I also landed a brace of small trout which, being a sportsman, I returned at once to the fins of their fretful mothers. The shoe I retained and brought home where I placed it alongside several boots, a single wellington, two iron hoops and a donkey's skull all of which had been taken by members of my family from the Feale River during their careers as fishermen. Years afterwards when I had grown more skilled as an angler I hooked and landed a dead cat at that part of the Feale known as the Corporal's hole. The cat, however, was too decomposed to be considered a legal catch and anyway he was nowhere like the three pound ten ounces tomcat taken by Thomas Moroney at an eddy near Finuge Bridge in the year 1968. This was the heaviest dead cat ever landed from the Feale. It broke a record which had lasted from nineteen hundred and nine, a total of fifty-nine years. This was a dead she-cat taken by a Constable Mortimer Wallace, a long since deceased R.I.C. man who had been stationed in the town in the early part of the century.

Wallace, who lived in Glounaphooka which ran parallel with the river, established other records which have not been equalled to this day. His most notable feat was the hooking and landing of a size forty-eight corset in nineteen hundred and eleven. A female acquaintance, an authority on this aspect of the clothing business, assures me that they don't make corsets of this size anymore. It was commonly believed at the time that the corset was the property of a fat woman who was a member of Hanratty's famous touring circus which called annually to Listowel and other country towns during the summer season.

Not long before Constable Wallace's arrival in Listowel a wise man who resided in Glounaphooka decided to keep records of notable and unusual catches from the fast-flowing Feale. The name of this wise man was Morisheen Bunce and when he died at the age of ninety-three he left his jotter of records to Paddy Carey who has faithfully made entries ever since and who is at all times willing and eager to display the book and its contents to those desirous of claiming records. I myself have seen the book and was overjoyed to note that on page forty-three under Section K was a record established by a relation of mine by the name of Dandy Keane. The same Dandy abandoned the Catholic Faith in the late twenties on the grounds that the crowds at mass and annual retreats made him nervous. He emigrated in nineteen thirty and joined some obscure Protestant Church in Canada which claimed only a handful of adherents. He died young in this persuasion.

In the book of records Dandy Keane was credited with landing the largest enamel chamber pot ever to be hooked by rod and line from one end of the Feale River to the other. I have no idea how many gallons it would contain but under the entry ran the following description: *Chamber Pot. Enamel Perforated at bottom. Handle attached. To hold water of twenty.* No mean achievement this when one looks at the puny, pint-sized, plastic chamber pots of today.

Experienced anglers may well ask what was the point in recording such catches when, as they maintain, there is no play involved. How wrong people can be. Believe me there is no play as satisfying as that which arises from the hooking of a size thirteen wellington in a boil of high water especially if the wellington is hooked at the top. Trying to land such a catch against a strong current of water calls for great strength and skill. Imagine trying too to land a ten gallon milk tankard or a five gallon bucket with line which has a mere breaking strain of ten or so pounds. This, in my humble estimation, is the ultimate in coarse angling.

In the jotter of records there are such varied catches as iron wheel bands, pantaloons, longjohns, ladies' knickers, hobnailed boots, skillet pots, saucepans, casseroles, overcoats, bicycle frames, horses' britching, saddles and harness not to mention every possible kind of ladies' and gents' apparel you care to mention.

We are indeed indebted to the late Morisheen

Bunce for instituting this roll of reliable records and should you dear reader live close by a stream or river you would be well thanked in time if you were to start this very day to record unusual and uncommon record catches so that posterity might appreciate the significant achievements of fishermen who forsook the common rut and neglected no aspect of angling.

BREAKING WIND

There have been numerous odes and essays devoted to the subject of wind-breaking. Alas most of these are in no way memorable and the rest, with a few notable exceptions, are so committed to vulgarity that it would be an insult to the good taste of my readers were I to quote from such foul calefactions. Everybody breaks wind. There are some who pretend they don't but the fact remains that we cannot always harness the tumult that thunders in the anus after unwise consumption of excessive food and drink. There are certain ladies whose fragile and angelic features would suggest that they are above such a lowly practice but, believe me, like truth the wind will out no matter how hard they try to suppress it.

Wind-breaking is a subject which polite people do not discuss. Alas this will not make wind-breaking go away. The ancient Greeks used to say that it was not by running away from evil that one overcame it but by going to meet it. Let readers bear this in mind. They should know by now that it is my wont to dwell upon all subjects under the sun and were I to overlook the practice of simple wind-breaking I would be unfaithful to my calling and disloyal to my readers.

Some time ago on my way through Limerick City I was suddenly overcome by thirst. I stopped near a well-known hostelry and wended my way towards this oasis of my choice. Seated at the bar counter was a small, curly-headed man whose face was somewhat familiar. He invited me to join him. I declined on the grounds that I was only having one due to the fact that I was in sole charge of a murderous machine called a motor-car. He seemed to take my refusal in good faith. I had little difficulty in attracting the barmaid's attention. She laid a glass she was polishing to one side and prepared herself to accept orders. As she did I took advantage of the diversion to make a closer study of the man who offered to buy me the drink. He had a weak face. A pencil thin moustache under a long, pointed nose was no asset in this respect. There was a general shiftiness about him, a hangdog look for which there is no real remedy.

I called for a pint, took a goodly swallow and savoured its nutritive and laving properties while I contemplated my second swallow. Then the unexpected happened. The small man, who was seated on a high stool, suddenly broke wind. I was taken completely by surprise. At first I thought it might have been a mere belch but there was no mistaking the note of anguish concealed in the release. It is this note, however faint, which distinguishes the breaking of wind from all oral pronouncements. There was no word of apology. He merely adjusted his buttocks and looked knowingly in the direction of the barmaid as if she were responsible. A nasty trick this, the last resort of knaves and tricksters. He smiled ingratiatingly in my direction to the accompaniment of an impuissance of staggered backfires. This time he looked at the barmaid with a mixture of reproof and reproach. She, blissfully unaware of the outside-the-counter activity, polished glass after glass with single-minded dedication. I wondered what her feelings might be if she knew she were being convicted in the wrong. She would be horrified I'm sure for no young lady, regardless of her station, would wish to be associated with underhand discharges of such a nature. The wind-breaker, cad that he was, smiled slyly and passed a meaningless remark about the weather. A silence ensued while I sat fearfully, praying that he would refrain from further utterances.

Then a very large, child-bearing lady entered holding a young girl by the hand. They sat themselves next to the wind-breaker. The senior member of the partnership addressed herself to the barmaid. Two glasses of orange with ice.

While they refreshed themselves the small man broke wind once more. The newcomer and her offspring looked up from their drinks startled and slightly shocked. There followed a long improvisation of lesser revelations of the posterus. The scoundrel looked in the direction of the child and on his face was the expression: 'It's alright, you can blame me. I'm a gentleman.'

Gulping their drinks hastily the mother and child departed the scene without as much as a whisper. The wind-breaker sipped his drink without reference to their exit. Here was a man who had reached a stage, through continuing deceit and self hypnosis, where he believed himself to be innocent of all hindmost hanky-pankiness. Here was a compulsive wind-breaker, incurable and unrepentant but then don't we, all of us, pretend that we do not see our faults and very often hide behind facades of self-righteousness.

But how does one recognise a typical wind-breaker? What are his classical points? Generally, alas, there is little to go by except for one outstanding characteristic. One would expect such a man to be restless, unable to sit still, to be forever adjusting and re-adjusting his rear end. Let me assure the innocent reader that the very opposite is the case. Your true, sneak-wind-breaker sits immobile and expressionless. There is never the slightest sign to suggest that he is the responsible party. Look for a man whose expression would suggest that wind-breaking is the last thought in his head and avoid him like you would a plague for deep under that seemingly innocent exterior is the potential for a thousand outbursts, long, short and medium.

Bearing this in mind I tried hard not to be disgusted with the fellow. Also to his advantage was the fact that I had declined to have a drink with him. Was his rearguard action an expression of disappointment and disillusionment with his fellow human beings? I had almost convinced myself that he was a victim of circumstances when he broke wind once more, this time with shattering effects. Even the barmaid reacted. The glass fell from her hand and shattered itself into fragments at her feet. Her pale features underwent an immediate change. In a thrice her face was as red as the proverbial beetroot. She dashed for cover with a cry like a stricken dove. Another long silence ensued at the end of which the barmaid emerged bashfully from some inner sanctum.

Then the wind-breaker arose and went towards the door. There he delivered his curtain line. It was addressed to me.

'You should try to remember,' said he, 'that there is a lady in the company.'

So saying he exited and left me stunned and embarrassed. I finished my drink, bowed as politely as I could to the barmaid and continued upon my journey. I should, of course, have left when he first opened fire. My mistake was that I gave the ruffian a second chance. Instead of redeeming himself he had betrayed me. I will never fall for such deception again. I will never trust a man with a face like his and I will react to any early backdoor delivery as would a sprinter to the crack of the starting pistol.

Later that night in the safety of my own bar I recounted my adventure to a number of sympathetic patrons. Each recalled similar experiences but one gentleman had a tale to tell in this respect which bears repeating. He was one day shooting pheasant in the County of Limerick with a titled lady who happened to be related to him. With them was a beater who had a reputation for diplomacy. As they made their way around the headlands of an October stubble-field a fine cock pheasant rose from a convenient thicket and presented an easy target. Alas the titled lady was taken by surprise and instead of firing a barrel she broke wind. She blushed for shame but the diplomatic beater came to her aid.

' Fire the second barrel my lady, ' said he, ' while the bird is still flying.'

YOUNG LOVE

The old believe everything, the middle-aged suspect everything, the young know everything.

Oscar Wilde

Sometimes in the pub at night the older members of the clientele bemoan the moral laxity of our time with special emphasis on the younger generation who would seem to be without inhibitions, scruples, conscience or the grace of God or at least this is the distinct impression an unbiased visitor might get if he happened to be holding a watching brief. Tales of murder, arson and rape are legion while ordinary misdemeanours such as theft, vandalism and disorderly conduct are no longer taken seriously. Drunkenness, sloth and unpunctuality would seem to be the chief distinguishing features of those who yearly teeter towards the terminations of their wanton teens while virtue of all kinds would no longer seem to be a thing to be sought after as a matter of course.

Others speak out in defence of youth and point out that this is a better generation than the last. The other night, however, an erudite gentleman, properly paunched and past his prime made a comparison between his time of heyday and now. He spoke, of course, from the entrenched position of age and property. He spoke with authority and with conviction and one would think to hear him pontificate that he was never a young man himself. As he recounted the wrongs perpetrated by the present generation his body trembled with barely-suppressed rage and self-righteousness. According to him there was never a time like the present time and he warned that continued vigilance was the only guarantee against the lot of us being murdered in our beds.

He maintained that nowadays women go around half-naked and, worst of all, wear no clothes at all in bed. A number of grey heads were seen to shake at this monumental revelation.

'You would think,' said he, 'that they would hould on to some stitch and not be making a holy show of themselves. My own wife,' he continued, 'wears her vest, her bloomers and her nightdress in bed not to mention a woollen cardigan if there's any touch of frost in the air.'

An older man in the company told him he should be truly thankful to have such a modest woman for a spouse.

'Women,' said he, 'that are only half-dressed are agents of the devil and if the law was the law all them that wears bikinis would be arrested.'

'Modern women,' said the properly-paunched man, 'couldn't boil an egg for you. But,' said he, 'they would do away with a bottle of vodka while you'd be looking around you. Then they go so far,' said he, 'as to make love with the lights on.'

'Oh, great God entirely,' said the older man, 'Can there be luck or grace where you have that sort of cary-out going on.'

In his time apparently this was unthinkeable and he went so far as to quote us a classical example of the vast void which separates then from now. An aunt of his, a comely and shy girl in her twenties, married herself to a neighbouring farmer for whom she had a great wish. After the wedding breakfast they did what all sensible couples do. They sought out a hotel in order to consummate the marriage. Mary went to bed first while Jack kept his back turned to her in case he might see anything. When Mary was safely between the sheets she covered her head so that Jack might undress himself. Need I say that Jack undressed himself in no time at all and made a buck-leap into the bed which would put the best efforts of a Thompson's Gazelle to shame. For awhile they lay side by side not daring to breathe. After awhile, however, nature asserted itself and they turned towards each other with affection and abandon.

We will not dwell on the details of the consummation. We will pass them over which is the proper thing to do and proceed to the morning. When Jack awoke he was astonished to discover that his young bride was nowhere to be seen.

He rose in a panic and was about to raise the alarm when he heard her dulcet voice assuring him that all was well from behind the closed door of the wardroble. He sat upon the side of the bed cogitating in full earnest. That she was alive and well there seemed to be no doubt whatsoever. What baffled him was why she should have transferred herself from a warm, comfortable bed to the dark and narrow confines of an uncomfortable wardrobe. The ways of country women are strange he told himself. Patience and understanding were two items which were sorely needed here.

'Why are you in the wardrobe?' asked Jack without the slightest shade of annoyance in his tone. At first no answer came so he repeated the question: 'Why are you in the wardrobe Mary dear?' he asked. After awhile the answer came back in a half-whisper:

'I'm here after last night,' said Mary.

'And what was wrong with last night?' Jack asked.

'Oh 'twas fine,' said she, 'but it was dark at the time whereas 'tis light now and I'm ashamed to show myself after what happened.'

Jack was a patient man. He coaxed her out after awhile and when she shyly complained about the light he drew the curtains and darkened the room. Our middle-aged friend was convinced that no modern bride would behave as did modest Mary. He went on to recount an incident of more recent vintage. It concerned a woman who was raped while she was cutting her corns. The guilty party was a lusty man who lived next door. Without a word of warning he came at her while she was paring her small toe. He did the foul deed and left silently by the back door. The first person the victim told was her mother. At first the mother was speechless. She sat on a convenient chair clutching her breast. After awhile her composure returned.

'Why didn't you resist?' said the mother.

'How could I?' said the daughter.

'Hadn't you a blade in your hand,' said the mother.

'It fell,' said the daughter, 'the minute he laid hands on me.'

'Why then didn't you screech?' asked the mother.

'Why didn't he screech?' said the daughter.

If we are to believe our middle-aged friend there is a vast moral divide between his time and ours. But wasn't it ever thus and it's a long time now since the first man posed the immortal question: 'What is the world coming to at all?' It's coming to an end of course and has been since it was first created. As we debated the rights and wrongs of the situation a newcomer entered and called for a half whiskey and a pint. He happened to hail from the nearby town of Glin which overlooks the mighty Shannon river as it cruises towards the Atlantic. He told us a refreshing story of youthful innocence. It restored our faith in human nature.

A young man not too far from Glin took a wife unto himself and spent the night of the honeymoon under the roof of his father's house. He did not appear for breakfast in the morning nor did he appear for lunch. In sensitive matters of this nature people pretend that everything is normal and that nothing untoward is taking place. They go about their business in the normal manner knowing from experience that sooner or later everything comes to an end. Consequently no comment was made regarding the young couple in bed. However, as the afternoon wore on the father and mother began to exchange apprehensive looks.

At this stage the father decided somewhat reluctantly to take action. He smote upon the bedroom door and announced to the son that the ware was on the table for the supper and it was time to rise and shine. Back came the son's answer without a moment's delay:

'Burn my clothes,' said he, 'I'm gettin' up no more.'

THE LOST ART OF CAPPING EGGS

Long ago when I was a boy, that is to say a real boy wearing short pants, with no interest in girls, the cap of a boiled egg was a much prized addition to the breakfast or supper of a growing girl or gorsoon. In those halcyon and innocent days eggs were not as plentiful as they are now but it is fair to say that an adult duck egg with a sufficiency of bread, butter and tea was enough to satisfy a grown man and a growing child for breakfast, dinner or supper as the case may be. Your adult duck egg was twice as large as your adult hen egg and a generous cap from one of these flavoursome, spheroidal orbs, the product of a mature duck, was as satisfying as a decent-sized sausage or a modest cube of pudding, black or white.

We are not here, however, to discuss the nutritious properties of hen eggs or duck eggs. We would be intruding upon the domains of others were we to do so. We are here instead to have a look at the lost art of egg-capping. There are, of course, countless ways of capping an egg and were I to recount all the known methods from Kentuckian to Tanganyikan we would fill most of this book.

I would ask prospective employers who chance to read this treatise to consider the egg-capping test as a means of assessing the merits of candidates for important positions. The candidates should be invited to a breakfast of boiled eggs. While they are engaged with the capping of a particular egg they should be observed closely. For instance a man who caps his egg with knife, spoon or other acceptable and orthodox capper, without first contemplating the contours and size of his egg, should be subject to automatic disqualification. Such an impetuous fellow will be no asset to an employer. ' Fools, ' said Pope, ' rush in where angels fear to tread,' and it should be obvious that a man who caps his egg without prior inspection is the kind of fellow who will rush headlong into delicate situations without primary investigation of any kind.

Another type of egg-capper who should be treated with suspicion is he who crushes the top of his egg with a single, savage blow of his spoon. In so doing he crushes the egg cap beyond repair making it extremely difficult to scoop out the cap's contents cleanly and without an unwanted interspersion of shell fragments. This candidate would be ideally suited to a job testing landmines but for any sort of delicate mission one would be better off with an elephant.

Bad as the aforementioned types are the most dangerous type of all is he who caps his egg without even looking. Here is a show-off, a man in search of instant success and glory, in reality a fellow who will involve his firm in serious trouble in the long run. Remember that no two eggs are alike either in shape or size and remember most important of all, that the texture of the shell in one egg may be able to endure several times the stress of the shell of another egg. In short the man who does not look while he caps can fall prey to any number of mishaps. To mention but one let us presume that his egg has been inadvertently boiled soft and that the texture of the shell is paper-thin as so often happens when least expected. He strikes the top of the egg casually and the next thing you know the soft yellow yolk is sent flying here, there and everywhere. Need I say more about the effect a thoughtless palooka like this might have on a decent firm trying to make its way in the world.

Here now is a portrait of the type of egg-capper who, in my estimation, would be ideally suited to a responsible job. Watch him closely when the egg is placed in front of him. His first action will be to address himself properly to his egg. His second act, if act it can be called, will be to survey the egg critically for several seconds, this to determine if it is an unusual or freakish spheroid or just another egg. His third act will be the most significant of all and here is where he will excel himself. He will lift the egg from the stand and hold it lightly in the palm of his hand for a moment or two judging its weight and general characteristics. He will then transfer it from one hand to the other, this in order to avail himself of a second opinion so to speak. Satisfying himself that no further advantage can be gained from handling his egg he will return it to its stand.

Now he will look to his implement of decapitation which in this case we will suppose to be a common spoon. This he will weigh carefully in the right hand only since this is the hand which will carry out the decapitation. Then decisively without further ado he will seize stand and egg together with the left hand gingerly tapping out a specific circle at the top of the egg. Inserting his spoon under this circle he will decisively remove the cap of the egg.

Here is your man for any position of trust and responsibility. Here, in the words of the poet, is your sound binocular.

Let us now look at other types of egg-cappers. We will begin with the most sensitive and delicate of all to wit, your ordinary, bald-headed man. It is a known fact that most bald-headed men spend more time capping the egg than they spend eating it. There is so much preliminary tapping and tipping that often the other occupants of the breakfast table have long finished wiping the yoke from their jaws and jowls before your hairless-pated, egg-prober commences his meal. This is because your bald-headed egg-capper imagines it is his own head which is on the block so to speak and for this reason he treats the smooth, bald top of the egg as though it were his own cranium.

By contrast your hard chaw with long, wild, uncontrollable hair makes a sudden and savage onslaught upon his egg. With no preamble of any kind he smites with the cup of his spoon on the top of the egg or on the bottom of the egg if this area is presented to him. In rural Ireland it was and still is looked upon as a bad omen if the bottom or narrower part of the egg is capped. Although I have questioned several mature countrymen at length there was none who could explain why the capping of the wrong side, as they called it, was destined to bring bad luck to the capper.

Not everybody uses an implement while capping an egg. The orthodox implements are, of course, knives or spoons or any other metal object which might be convenient. Some outdoor types whose hands have been calloused and hardened beyond sensitivity by the nature of their work merely tap the egg against the kitchen floor until it is properly fractured. It is then a simple matter to remove the cap by employing the thumb and the index finger to sever it with a minimum of force from the body of the egg. I have seen men of this ilk tap the egg against their foreheads, against the soles or heels of their shoes and sometimes against their heads. It is of no matter really so long as the top of the egg is sufficiently fractured to facilitate easy removal of the cap.

Those of us who like a boiled egg regularly will have little difficulty in capping our eggs with reasonable success. Practice may not always make perfect but it helps and there are some of us who could cap our eggs blindfolded provided they were not too soft. Your soft egg is the hardest of all to decapitate. Great care must be taken from the outset unless we are to have trails of yolk defacing the sides of our egg. In-depth capping of soft eggs can be disastrous and the safest course is to remove only that amount of shell which will leave enough space for the entry of an egg spoon. Some wily egg-eaters when dealing with soft eggs fracture the top of the egg and remove the shell from the fractured area with the fingers. They then remove the naked top of the egg with the spoon. To my way of thinking this is not a very sporting method. However, none of us are born egg-cappers and we must begin somewhere.

The best way to induct a newcomer such as a toddler to the art of egg-capping is to start him off on eggshells. This can be done by the simple expedient of turning the empty shell upside down in the eggstand. There is no danger that ill-luck will accrue since the shell is empty and cannot be said to be a whole or legitimate egg. After four or five years practising on upturned eggshells the youngster in question is certain to acquire reasonable proficiency and may be trusted under supervision to cap his own egg. Maximum proficiency comes only with adulthood and even then I would be loth to trust soft-boiled eggs to those who might be under the influence of alcohol or who may be suffering from nervous disorders.

AUGUST THOUGHTS

A man once told me that bulls are at their worst in August because the end of the love season is in sight and anyway all their energies have been dissipated due to intemperate devotion to consenting cows and hederaceous heifers across the sensuous days of summer. I daresay the same could be said of other creatures gifted with greater intelligence but let us ignore these and look at Autumn as a whole. Surely there is more to it than lovesick bulls and ingratiating heifers.   Autumn, of course, is that tranquil and even-tempered state which stands between those arch enemies winter and summer.   Personified he would look like a well-fed, middle-aged man who in his summer knew all the excesses. Balding now, paunchy, tolerant, he awaits the coming of winter when like all his kind he must finally expire or as Shakespeare so eloquently put it:

> He has his winter too of pale misfeature
> Or else he would forego his mortal nature.

Presently, of course, there are many intelligent people who believe that Shakespeare was really a Kerryman who left Ballybunion after the disastrous August week-end of fifteen eighty. How else could he make so many fine utterances regarding nature unless he spent a *tamaill* in the Kingdom.

I believe that if man could accept his nature as he does the seasons he would be better resigned to accept death but enough of this doleful deliberating. Let us look instead to familiar and unfamiliar aspects of August. For some as the nights grow colder it means merely a change-over from beer to stout, preference having been extended to the lighter draught during the soporific nights of summer whereas to others all autumn suggests is the substitution of long-johns and allied woollens for summer shorts and singlets. To others it means the gradual discoloration of that area of the anatomy which was exposed to burning sun and warm wind while the summer sun was generous. To a bachelor who resides between Knockanure and Athea it means another notch on a holly cudgel which hangs over his hearth. It is not to signify another conquest nor the registering of another year. It is merely to herald the arrival of another weary, womanless winter, the twenty-fifth of its kind, etched on the vellum-like bark of the holly-butt, since he first proposed to and was rejected by a succession of marriageable women. Autumn for him spells a silent kitchen, a poor table and a cold bed.

My fondest memories of august are the pattern days which fell on August fifteenth. The most famous of these was the Ballybunion Pattern which attracted thousands of visitors from north Cork, west Limerick and all over Kerry. Traditionally it was the day-out of the farmers' boys and farmers' girls who would insist at the start of the year that the fifteenth was to be free. Mostly they came on cycles and in pony traps. The buses too brought hundreds and what a sight it was to see the girls in their figures parading up and down the Main Street munching buns and sucking ice-creams and peeking into public houses wondering would the men never come out to dance in the streets. There was every kind of a huckster. One I remember best of all. He stood on the Castle Green with a large suitcase at his feet. He sold bottles of lotion for the sum of one shilling per half-pint. One and nine for double size. According to the label the mixture would ' painlessly eradicate spots and other blemishes from ladies' bellies.' He did a roaring trade. The whole meaning of this and other patterns was the bidding of a formal goodbye to summer-time, a sort of last fling before the days grew short.

I myself am made aware of the end of August by the mounting anxiety in the frenzied communications of the swallow colonies in the many sheds and outhouses in the backway at the rear of my house. It is as if they were building up courage for the long flight to winter quarters. There is the endless twittering as the days grow shorter and time starts to run out. Soon the twittering will be feverish in its discontent as they convey to each other the necessity for immediate departure to warmer climes.

Then I wake one morning and the twittering is no more. There is a vacuum that sparrows or rooks cannot fill and I know for sure that with the swallows' leavetaking the first advice note for winter has arrived.

Some of my readers may not have heard of the famous bog of Dirha which lies between Listowel and Ballybunion. The arrival of autumn to Dirha Bog is an occasion of great significance. Sonny Canavan's goat herd, swollen beyond belief by the advent of countless kids has turned that area of the bog where they are currently grazing into a slowly-moving, speckled mass from which comes the interminable bleating of young kids and lovelorn she-goats. There is a new puck in the herd. Canavan has christened him Paisley not because he resembles the political cleric in any physical way but because the animal in question is due to be exported very soon on account of the unrest he is causing in the herd. The wild heather is now at its purpliest and the turf ricks line the white, dusty roadway turning it into a brown-walled avenue. The snipe are back and one can see them whirring and darting all over the sky whenever humanity intrudes upon their sedgy confines. Curlews will soon circle above the purple banks, mournfully keening the death of another gallant August. For my own part I look forward to September since it is my favourite month. Its crisp air and indescribable colouring appeal most to me without discounting the inevitable floods, so rich, deep and restrained. But back to Dirha Bog.

Sonny Canavan and I walk slowly along the asspassage counting the goats. He is endeavouring to select an outstanding she-goat for a special bodhrawn order. I am reminded by his speech of its close affinity to Shakespeare's many fine utterances on so many difficult subjects. A business-man passed by on the outer road. He had his hands behind his back and on his head he wore a hat.

'I wouldn't be under that hat,' said Canavan, 'for all the tea in China.'

'Why not?' I asked.

'Because,' said Canavan, 'there's no rest under it'.

Had not William Shakespeare in his time said the same thing exactly when he wrote: 'Uneasy lies the head that wears a crown.'

A nip starts to come into the air because whatever about autumn days, autumn nights are sprinkled with frost and evening was slowly approaching from the distant hill of Cnocanore.

Another man passed in a pony-rail. He was a hoary-headed fellow who had in his heyday a reputation for rutting as good if not better than any of Canavan's pucks. This particular old reprobate hailed a few cycling girls who had a good giggle at him.

'He thinks he's as young as he used to be,' said Canavan, 'but he couldn't perform now no more nor a carcass.'

In *Henry the Fourth,* Shakespeare's celebrated classic we have something similar:

'Is it not strange that desire should so many years outlive performance.'

What an awful pity that Shakespeare and Canavan never met. I suggested this to Canavan. 'By the

Gingo,' said he, 'you'd have ferocious tatarara.'

We spoke about Listowel Races and Canavan reminded me of the time when a man would be sparing every halfpenny he could lay his hands on from the end of June and thinking up countless ways of making a few shillings. In Sonny's youth every working man would have a rick of turf for sale at the end of the summer or maybe a few fat pigs or calves or a lone bullock or heifer. If not there would be a few butts of good spuds or a few rails of turnips, in fact anything that would swell the purse so that it lasted till the week of the races was over. Canavan conceded that while the crowds of revellers were presently far smaller on race-nights there was now more comfort, more peace and more money.

'Blast me,' said Canavan, 'when I was a young man I wouldn't have a crubeen in my hand during a race night when it would be knocked out of it by some ignorant cawbogue on top of dirty sawdust.'

Here again other immortal lines come to mind, not Shakespeare's this time but James Payne's:

> I never had a piece of toast
> Particularly long and wide
> But fell upon the sandy floor
> And always on the buttered side.

No doubt there's nothing new under the sun. As we talked the sun dropped and the sky grew pale in true August style. The moon developed slowly and as it did we were approached by a man who wanted to buy a goat for the purpose of making a bodhrawn. Canavan stated his price but the would-be purchaser found it too dear. He told us that he could steal goats if he wanted to without fear of being caught but that he was as honest as ever drew breath. He then departed. Canavan watched him go and shook his head ruefully;

'The minute he said he wouldn't steal goats,' said Canavan. 'I started to count mine.'

Upon hearing this I recalled similar sentiments contained in a famous couplet, the name of whose author just now escapes me:

> The louder he talked of his honour,
> The faster we counted our spoons.

BIG WORDS

Most of our English teachers warned us at one time or another of the folly arising from the use of a big word where a small one would do just as well. Be this as it may, however, there was nothing so deflating to an ignoramus or common thug as a barrage of well-timed, well-spaced, multi-syllabic tongue-twisters. Backward and suspicious folk unversed in the subtleties and sonorousness of sublime expression have a healthy respect for the man who has words at will and will give him a wide berth for fear of invoking his wrath. In fact there are many sensible country people who would much prefer a lick of a naked fist.

The worst a belt of this nature can do is give you a black eye or a broken jaw either of which can be cured and forgotten about altogether in the course of time. Not so with a nicely mounted cluster of sharp, scintillating words. These can leave scars and sores that will not heal for a genesis of generations. How many will disagree that an absurd sobriquet has twice the punishing powers of a comprehensive physical beating. The old Gaelic chieftains had a greater fear of satire and ridicule than of sworn enemies out for a man's blood. At least you could build castles against your enemies but against the invective of a disgruntled bard there was no defence whatsoever and even if you cut off his head before he got started one of his brotherhood was sure to lambast you with a lacerating and lineage-defiling displode which was sure to be remembered unto the third and even the fourth generation.

Anything was preferable to the poet's curse or the wit's tag and if 'twas the last forkful of meat in the house itself it was wiser to part with it rather than risk the wrath of a starving poetaster.

Worse still, of course, was to be fettered by a mouthful of words which the benighted victim would have no hope of understanding. Bad as he is the devil one knows is better than the devil one does not know and what an ordeal to have to go through the world like a dog with a cannister tied to its tail.

There are others, of course, notably schoolboys, who have no fear whatsoever of the spoken word when delivered by a disgruntled teacher. The longer the tirade the less likelihood of physical punishment. The maxim here was:

> Sticks and stones may break my bones,
> But words will never hurt me.

However, I remember a singular exception to this. Many years ago in Listowel there was a secondary teacher by the name of Paddy Breen who was reputed to be one of the best English scholars in Kerry. Once after an argument with an inspector he was asked by the school's President to render an account of what happened.

'All that happened,' said Paddy, 'was that I bade the fellow beat an ignominious retreat to the native valleys of his own obscurity.'

There was in Paddy Breen's heyday a pupil attending the school who arrived each morning unfailingly late. Always he would come up with a different excuse. It so happened that one morning Paddy was taking the first class of the day. Our friend, as was his wont, arrived a half hour late.

'Well,' said Paddy, 'what excuse have you to offer this time?'

'My mother's watch sir she stopped,' was the inventive answer. All the other clocks and watches in the house had long since been rendered inoperable due to a variety of misfortunes.

'You sir,' said Paddy Breen, 'are the misbegotten metamorphosis of a miscalculating microchronometer.'

Our young friend took the jibe poorly and did not attend class the following day nor indeed for many a day afterwards. Eventually Paddy received a solicitor's letter asking him if he would be good enough to repeat the damaging statement in court. Paddy replied that he would be agreeable and sent the solicitor an exact copy of what he said. No more was heard of the matter but had he used smaller and more easily understood words there would have been no misunderstanding whatsoever. Alas there would have been no colour either and the class would have been a drabber, duller place. Readers then may gather that I do not altogether agree with teachers who lay too much stress on simplicity. All the words in the dictionary are there to be used and every word no matter how discumbumbulating it may be deserves an airing now and then. A sameness of small or undistinguished words will definitely present a practical and clear picture but they will not alas present a memorable picture with, of course, the honourable exceptions such as Four Ducks in a Pond and the like which only serve to prove my point.

BED HERMITS

One Monday morning a neighbour complained to me that she could not get her daughter out of bed. I cited for her an ancient cure for this now-uncommon malady.

There was a time when every community boasted at least one bed hermit, that is to say a person who took to the bed and stayed there over the years in spite of the fact that no sickness was apparent. These bed hermits are less common nowadays for the good reason that they cannot find people to look after them. This task was usually allotted to elderly spinsters and other timid creatures who lived in constant dread of the great outdoors for reasons best known to themselves.

I personally remember a postman from my early youth. He was wrongfully accused of purloining a sixpenny postal order from one of the letters entrusted to his care. He was dismissed and was allowed to remain in this woeful state of criminal suspension until it accidentally came to light some weeks afterwards that an error had been made. When his superior called to see him he was not admitted to the house. The postman's sister informed the official that her brother had taken to bed the day he was dishonourably discharged and had not left it except for basic purposes in the interim. Others called in an attempt to dissuade him from the bed but all to no avail. Thirty years were to pass before he would again reveal himself in public.

He was one of several bed hermits of my acquaintance. The most notable lived three miles away in the countryside. Some years before at the age of eighteen she took to the bed and stoutly refused to budge even when her irate parents threatened to burn the bed upon which she lay. All fruit failed, however, and when all fruit fails we must try haws, the haw in this case being a black doctor who visited the town of Listowel for one week in the year during Listowel races and plied his venerable trade in the market place.

His name was Doctor Curio. I remember him well. He was of Nigerian extraction and was as black as the proverbial ace of spades or blacker than a famine spud as they still say in these parts. He wore a tall hat and a swallowtail coat. He operated from a small bamboo table upon which were placed a few dozen of his internationally famous Curio's Cure-All. This incredible mixture sold at the modest price of two shillings a bottle and it differed from conventional doctors' bottles in that it could be used externally as well as internally.

Doctor Curio boasted that it also exterminated fleas. It could be used for the treatment of blisters, craw-sickness and carbuncles as well as for the eradication of warts, welts, vertigo and all female disorders. It was without peer as a liniment and was guaranteed to banish cramps, sprains and strained muscles when properly applied.

Doctor Curio, according to his credentials, was a graduate of the university of Walla Walla which, for undisclosed reasons, was not to be found on any African maps of the time.

When the good doctor was approached by the parents of the female bed hermit he listened carefully to what they had to say. Having digested everything of relevance he asked a most pertinent question. How much was in it for him? After a certain amount of haggling in which neighbours of the parents, the fattest woman in the world and a pair of three-card-tricksters were involved, a fee of five pounds, an enormous sum at the time, was agreed upon.

Duly the black doctor arrived at the abode of the recluse. A large and curious crowd had gathered to witness the miracle. Doctor Curio first demanded the fiver which was handed over to him at once. He then ordered all the occupants of the house to remove themselves from its vicinity. This they did and with the neighbours and others stood at a respectful distance awaiting developments.

When the black doctor entered the bedroom the first thing he did was to remove his hat. He then politely suggested to the lady in the bed that it might be best if she abandoned it. This she refused to do. Instead she pulled the clothes tightly around her and stuck out her tongue at Doctor Curio. He decided to ignore this monstrous irreverence. Without a word he removed his coat and placed it at the foot of the bed. Only then did the first look of alarm cross the bed hermit's face. Calmly the doctor removed his waistcoat, shirt and vest and a string of shark's teeth which happened to be tied around his belly to protect him against evil spirits.

The bed hermit was now sitting up in the bed, a look of absolute panic having replaced the one of alarm. Calmly the black man started to take off his trousers. This was too much for the lady in the bed. With a frightful screech she threw back the clothes and fled through the front door, her nightdress trailing behind her. She ran past the astounded audience shrieking at the top of her voice. Fully dressed the great Doctor Curio appeared in the doorway. He lifted his hat to his audience and returned to take up his rightful position in the market place.

The lady in question never took to the bed again. Neither did she reveal the methods which the black doctor employed to eject her.

SKILLET POTS

> In a big ocean liner I'm sailing in style
> I'm sailing away from the Emerald Isle.

So opens the nostalgic ballad *Cutting the Corn* which deals with the departure of a young Donegal man from his native Creeslough for the far-off shores of America. From start to finish it is a touching refrain but we will not concern ourselves with the lonelier side of the situation. Instead we will deal with a particular aspect, to wit a couplet dealing with stirabout pots and which runs something like this:

> Sure I swear to you Danny I'd swap the whole lot,
> For the ould wooden spoon and the stirabout pot.

Even allowing for poetic licence we may presume that Danny's friend was deeply attached to the skillet or rather to the contents of the skillet. We may also presume that the young men of those far-off times, after returning from late-night dances, made directly for the skillet just as today's young men make directly for the fridge.

I may not have the words exactly right but

accuracy is not essential in this case so there is no need for readers to write in correcting me. It would be a waste of stamp, paper and envelope constituting altogether another minor setback to the economy.

An approximation of the sentiment involved will serve our stirabout pot or as it is more familiarly known, the skillet pot. Indeed there is a delightful ballad devoted to this revered utensil the chorus of which goes like this:

> Oh weren't they the happy days
> When troubles we had not
> And our mothers made Colcannon
> In the little skillet pot.

There are several other important musical compositions also relating to the skillet, all complimentary except for one in which the skillet is used to crack a man's head.

The skillet was also less poetically referred to as the Gruel Vessel. Gruel and stirabout were one and the same thing with ground maize as the base and being the staple diet of most of the people of rural Ireland for many years after Black Forty-Seven. Maize was also used in the making of yellow meal or 'Pake' pointers but since these belong in another province to wit the griddle we will not dwell thereon longer than we have to. Nowadays skillet pots are used for ornamental purposes only and in a sense I am glad for they might serve to remind us of times when hunger was the predominant fear of Irish households. In a sense I daresay the skillet pot has outlived its usefulness and could hardly be regarded as an ideal companion for the sophisticated foodstuffs of today. One of the great advantages of the skillet was its compactness and yet as a container it was most deceptive for it could hold as much food as certain other utensils which looked twice its size. Another powerful advantage was that it was made completely from iron, its cover included. This latter was a weighty object and unlike the compressed covers of other pots and saucepans which were largely tin and aluminium (no disrespect intended) great pressure was required if it was to be lifted from the parent pot. Lifted, however, it often was to allow the escape of what I will refer to as unnatural gases. These gases are the sole support of indigestion, dyspepsia, flatulence and all the other gaseous incumbents to which the human belly is heir. These gases abound in every stomach in great numbers and their discontented, volcanic-like rumblings are often an embarrassment to their owners. Some gases merely gurgle whilst others erupt into mighty belches. Other gases miaow like kittens while still more rumble and mumble like distant thunder. All these stomach utterances were once collectively classified under the general title of 'Wind', surely a euphemism, if ever there was one. Wind is a purifier whereas gas is a polluter. Of itself wind has no odour whereas gases, particularly the ones in question, have. The moment the cover of the skillet is lifted by these internal powerful vapours it automatically falls back into place again, thereby retaining the natural and nutritive, harmless gases which are fulsome and flavoursome and expelling forever those invisible but poisonous substances which have been the ruin, over the years, of innumerable stomachs.

Let me put it another way. If a gas is so potent that it can pressurise an iron cover into lifting itself, even for an instant, from its sole support we may well consider with alarm the effect this gas would have on an unsuspecting stomach. I am not suggesting that the skillet is the panacea for all stomach ailments. What I am suggesting is that the skillet pot is not a deceiver of the digestive tract like many others we could mention. I'll state no names but I will donate a prize to the first person who resurrects a worthwhile ballad about a frying pan.

Those who know me will concede that, for all my faults, I am not a man to make pronouncements lightly. When I do I am buttressed by solid evidence which I can produce at a moment's notice. I can cite examples too at the drop of a hat. The following will do nicely.

When I was a youth in the Stacks Mountains there returned to the land of his birth from the city of New York a long-term exile whose christian name was Patrick. He was immediately re-christened Patcheen the Yank. He endeared himself to all and sundry with an expression he was fond of using in public houses. The expression was purely and simply: 'The drinks is on me.' This drew him many friends and sympathisers and when, after a few weeks of heavy boozing, his stomach started to react, there was concern far and wide for his well being. There were other Yanks in the neighbourhood who came and went and who suffered illnesses of one kind or another but nobody, saving their immediate kinfolk, were greatly put out. Patrick was a different kettle of fish. Here was a good-natured, gullible fellow possessed of more than adequate coin of the realm. Should his position deteriorate it would mean that he would have no means of spending his money.

When he fell sick it was felt at first that it was a mere minor illness brought about by the change of climate.

However, when he failed to appear in his favourite haunts after a period of three weeks his countless friends began to grow seriously worried. They wondered what could be wrong with him. The cause of Patcheen the Yank's setback was, of course, that his diet had been consistently liquid from the moment of his arrival in the old country. Often in his cups he would mourn the friends of his youth and the death of ancient customs. Now and then he would wistfully refer to the colcannon his dear departed mother would hold hot for him in the family skillet. It was an easy matter to make the colcannon. For a beginning he was given a bit out of his hand, that is to say a small saucerful or plateful. It worked wonders. His stomach healed itself in no time and he was, I am happy to say, quickly back to his old habit of saying 'the drinks is on me'.

CANAVAN'S DOG

It must be five or six years now since I last made mention of Canavan's talking dog, Banana the Sixth. In response to numerous letters from readers over this period I am happy to assure them that all is well with this remarkable canine. Banana is now in his tenth year and from time to time is given to those priceless utterances which have made him justly famous. The other night as he and Canavan sat by the fire the dog's attention was caught by a report which appeared on the back page of a paper which Canavan happened to be reading. He placed one of his paws on the column and indicated to Canavan that he would appreciate it if the contents of the report were read out to him. Canavan obliged. The dog, as everybody knows, is illiterate although a fluent speaker in both Irish and English. At the head of the column was a photograph of a man and a dog and this was what claimed Banana's interest.

It transpired that the report was an obituary notice on the famous American conman, Joseph Yellow-Kid Weill. The dog was one of Weill's internationally known talking dogs although people who purchased the dogs claimed that immediately afterwards the mutts were permanently stricken with laryngitis. This may have been true to some extent since Weill was a competent ventriloquist.

Canavan's dog nodded his head and wagged his tail when his master concluded, a sure sign that he was about to make a major pronouncement which he promptly did.

'That dog,' said he indicating the one with Weill, 'is a cousin of mine.'

'How can that be?' Canavan asked, 'when none of your seed or breed was ever in America?'

'My dear man,' said the dog, 'my late ancestor, Banana the First, had a sister called Spot who was pressganged aboard a rat-infested coffin-ship for the sole purpose of disposing of the rats in question. She never returned to her native Lyreacrompane because nobody would give her a passage home to the Land of Slugs and Dossers. Instead of dying of a broken heart which any ordinary bitch would have done she instead mated herself to a one-eyed Yukonian watchdog who was three-eights wolf, one-eight Alsatian, one-eight Elkhound and three-eights Kerry Blue. Of issue there was but one male who went on to father the only known American family of talking dogs. This dog, therefore, which you see before you is a blood cousin of mine. Need I say more.'

'Fair enough,' said Canavan, knowing that it was useless arguing with the dog when he struck a vein like this. The pair sat silently in front of the fire watching the flames as they flickered in the ancient hearth. Outside a curlew called and in the distance a dog barked. Deep in the bog a lost ass brayed long and low and a mating bittern bleated romantically.

'You referred there,' said Canavan, 'to the land of Slugs and Dossers when you must have meant the land of Saints and Scholars.'

'Slugs and Dossers is what I said,' Banana the Sixth announced firmly, 'and Slugs and Dossers is what I meant. Is it a country where men who won't work and who were used only to ass and cars ten years ago have now fine motor-cars? Is it a country where men earning several thousand pounds a year are looking for more when old-age pensioners are expected to live on a fraction of that? Looking for more imagine and they having plenty already. Is it a country where they won't show up for work and where doctors' certs are as common as bogwater?'

'Now, now,' said Canavan, 'you'll give us a pain so you will.'

'Don't mind your now, now,' said Banana the Sixth, 'don't you see them yourself resting in their motor-cars and they reading papers when they should be working? Don't you see them at everything except the job they're getting paid to do? There is no work being done in this country at the present time. Don't I see them going down that very road outside to the bog and they wearing low shoes and collars and ties. What country could stick that kind of carry-on? It couldn't last. No country could carry so many dodgers and survive for long. A nation of Slugs and Dossers is what I said and a nation of Slugs and Dossers is what I meant.'

So saying the dog rose and went out into the haggard where he addressed himself to the moon which was in the last quarter. He howled high and clear until a band of ragged clouds came from the direction of Ballybunion and hid Diana in their midst. The dog went indoors and sat in his favourite place near the hearth. Canavan put out the lights and went to bed.

THE LOST HEIFER

I remember a white heifer which was driven to town in the company of two other heifers by a small farmer close on two score years ago. He was forced to sell them because of pure impoverishment. He entered the square of Listowel exhausted and bedraggled after a journey of five hours from the foothills of the Stacks Mountains. It was only seven miles but this was good time when you consider that he had three recalcitrant heifers under his command.

To assist him in this marathon cattle drive he had a ready gorsoon of twelve or so and a small lean, underfed dog of indeterminate strain. The gorsoon was his son, a useful lad with his legs, able to move with speed and precision whenever the heifers abandoned the roadway for the familiarity of adjacent fields. No toll much was taken out of the youth. It was the dog and his master who suffered. The dog was never properly trained and whenever he exceeded his duties by misdirecting or snapping at the cattle he fell in for, you guessed it, dog's abuse. The farmer himself was far from being fit. Fear of hunger and overwork left him without the hardiness essential for the successful hustling of heifers over mountainy roads.

The trio of man, boy and dog managed to corral

the heifers in a corner of the square. Here they stood them until jobbers saw fit to inspect them. In transactions of this nature and period it was every man for himself. Backward farmers, unaware of the fluctuations in the market, were often forced to sell cheaply and prematurely rather than be left with cattle on their hands which seldom happened in all truth but there was the danger and it was a trump card the jobber never failed to play.

Our man from the Stacks Mountains had little difficulty in disposing of two of his herd but as the day wore on it seemed less and less likely that he would be able to find a buyer for the white heifer. At the time the farmers of Ireland had little *meas* in white cattle. They were called bawnies and were notoriously slow to develop. Fair-haired or blond people were often nicknamed bawnies when one wanted to imply disparagement.

As the evening wore on our friend would repair now and then to the nearest pub where he would order and consume a medium of stout or maybe two if he chanced to run across an acquaintance. Earlier he had invested in a bag of buns and a bottle of lemonade for the son. Buns were looked upon as luxuries in those days and shown more veneration than fresh meat, sausages or black puddings. In the heel of the evening the dog wandered off after a passing bitch. The youngster, drowsy from the early rising and the long trek of the morning, fell fast asleep where he sat on the kerb. In the pub the boy's father forgot the woes which had ground him down all the year. He swallowed medium after medium of stout until someone reminded him that it would be dark soon and that it would be as gay for him to be chancing the road home. Reluctantly he left the dreamland of sawdust, barrels and bottles and made his way to the corner of the square where he had last seen his heifer, his dog and his son. There was no heifer to be seen. The dog was no great loss. Dogs could be had for the asking but a heifer, even though white, was a different matter altogether. His first act was to wake his offspring. His second was to present him with a box in the ear, this to refresh his memory regarding his last waking impressions of the vanished heifer. The youngster alas had no idea where the animal had strayed. The procedure for dealing with missing cattle in those days always followed a ritualistic pattern. First there was a visit to the Guards' Barracks where the orderly would promise to do his best to locate the animal. This done the next step was to a central newsagent who would display a description of the strayaway on his front window for a modest sum, generally in the region of a three-penny piece. The next step was the schools. In most towns there was a National School for boys and another for girls. There might also be corresponding secondary schools. The visits to the schools was another day's work and anyway there was always a fair chance that they might encounter the heifer on the way back home. This, however, they failed to do.

The following day the man from the Stacks

Mountains mounted his bicycle and headed for the town. It was a wet and windy day but this did not deter him. First he called to the barracks but there was no word there. He tried the boys National School before the others for the simple reason that he had once attended such an establishment himself although without any degree whatsoever of success. He tried each class in turn and ended up in ours which in Oriental parlance might be termed the Class of the Sixth Book.

Here the teacher received him courteously. Then in his own words he gave a description of the heifer:

'She war a narra Bawnie,' he informed us. 'She war stone mad on top of it and she have only a horn and a half.'

Several hands shot up and their owners clamoured for attention. The teacher ignored them. He knew they were only budding Thespians who hungered for the limelight.

When the initial clamour had died the teacher repeated the description. Two hands shot up.

'Where did you see her?' the teacher asked of the first.

'Sir, I can't remember the place but if I was took there I'd remember it.'

'Sit down,' said the teacher. Here, he knew, was a dodger looking for the rest of the day off. The teacher questioned the second boy who provided an accurate description of a bohareen where he had seen the heifer that morning.

The face of the man from the Stacks Mountains

lighted up. When he had first entered the classroom, wearing his black coat tied with an outsized safety pin at the throat, he looked like a corpse with his ashen face and his dark curly hair hanging wet from under his drenched cap. He carried an ashplant and his coat was bound round with a length of homemade hayrope. His dripping trousers were thrust inside his turned-down wellingtons and round him, where he stood, pools of water were forming on the floor.

Looking back now he looked the very personification of the blighted thirties, a beaten man but a man who refused to give in. It's no wonder farmers are doing well today. God owes it to them from the days of the Economic War and the hungry years that followed since.

FOOD DRESSINGS

Recently with a business acquaintance I spent a night in Dublin. By extraction he is a countryman from a hinterland area but he is a man who likes value for money and likes his pleasures to be simple and unadorned. He is also a man of few words but those few are so well taken and carefully thought out that they are far more effective than the sum total of the jabberings of a registered loudmouth. I will say no more about the man except that he is a true friend, a thorough gentleman and a good judge of whiskey.

The foregoing information should be sufficient to provide interested parties with an adequate insight into his character. Were I to say more we would have the beginnings of a biography and nobody wants that, neither me, you, nor the man in question. Now to the purpose of our treatise which has to do with tomatoes and lettuce and things of that nature. Perhaps I should say here and now that there are parts of this country where tomatoes, lettuce and the likes never quite took on, parts where they are regarded with suspicion and curiosity or at best looked upon as comparative and unworthy newcomers to the kitchen table.

It is important to make this clear now if we are to

avoid misunderstanding later. Let us at once, therefore, continue with our narrative. When my friend and I came downstairs we made straight for the dining-room where we were ushered to a table by a bright faced waitress who immediately presented us with two menus. The offerings thereon were modest but satisfactory. There was bacon and egg, bacon and sausage, bacon and liver. There were poached eggs, boiled eggs and scrambled eggs. Had there been no alternative to the eggs we would have been in a pretty pucker. After a brief surveillance I opted for bacon and liver and my friend declared for bacon and sausages.

We had not long to wait. In less than ten minutes the waitress was beaming by our sides and placing warm plates under our noses. I dived in straight away and was masticating my second mouthful when I noticed my friend was not eating.

'What's up?' I asked.

'Everything is up,' said he. Then he pointed to his plate. I inspected it and could only ascertain that it contained the same ingredients as my own except that he had sausages and I had liver. On his plate there were two small rashers, two semi-detached sausages of medium size and one other detached sausage of similar symmetry. There was a small slice of tangerine-coloured tomato and there was a large leaf of disaffecting lettuce.

'I fail to see anything wrong,' I said.

'That's because you're a townie,' he said, 'and townies would eat anything.' So saying he banged on the table and summoned the waitress. By this time he was pale-faced with anger and impatiently tapping his side plate with his upturned fork. The waitress arrived.

'Yes, sir?' she said.

'What did I order?' he asked.

'You ordered bacon and sausages sir,' the girl said.

'Correct,' said he, 'and tell me did I order a leaf of lettuce and a slice of unripe tomato?'.

'Them is only dressings sir,' she said with a laugh. This seemed to infuriate him further. He ordered her to remove the offending items from the plate and to return it with bacon and sausages only. The girl did as she was bade and when she had replaced the plate he addressed her as follows:

'Have a good gander at my kisser,' said he, 'so that you will recognise me the next time I come into this dining-room. When I order bacon and sausages it means bacon and sausages and not with tomato and lettuce. Tomatoes and lettuces is for townies.' Upon conclusion of this harangue he turned his attention to his plate to see if there was any trace of lettuce or tomato remaining. There was none. He set to eat at once but consumed a few morsels only. He explained that the sight of the lettuce and tomato had seriously affected his appetite.

'I can't bear the sight of them,' he said.

Outrages like the aforementioned are the fault of hoteliers. I have often myself been the victim and was once served fish with two slices of lemon on top of it. I dislike lemon except in hot whiskey yet the hotel had the gall to serve me with it without having been invited to do so. I asked the waitress to take the plate back and to have the lemon removed.

'That's what your side plate is for,' she said.

That was my compensation. The fish had already been contaminated by the lemon so I left it there. On another occasion I was having a meal with two elderly ladies in a well-known hotel. One ordered cold meat. With it she got a large slice of beetroot and a leaf of lettuce both of which she loathes. We called the waitress and asked her what was the idea.

'Dressing,' she said.

'If you don't mind,' said the old lady, 'I like to do my own dressing.'

I daresay the same applies to everybody so no more dressings please except at the request of the customer.

MIXED GRILLS

I have a dream. It is to write a thesis on the mixed grill before progress reduces it to an absurdity. This would be the definitive work on the subject. It would be found after Mixed Enterprise (Econ) in *The Encyclopaedia Britannica*. When my name would crop up people would ask what's he done that's so important? There would be a shocked silence from the erudite after which would come the confidential whisper briefly outlining my single achievement. The name Keane would be synonymous with the mixed grill. When I would pass by a crowd people would say reverently and proudly: 'There goes Keane, the mixed grill man.' I would be introduced as Mister Mixed Grill himself. In my obituary notice there would be mention of my most notable achievement. 'Keane was the man,' it would read, 'who rescued the mixed grill from oblivion.' My descendents would come to be known as The Mixed Grill Keanes. That is my dream. I often ask myself if it exceeds my rightful expectations but no answer comes. I believe, however, that it is my destiny. Some men were born to free sewerage pipes, others to pick plums. I was born to write about mixed grills. This is not my first time. I have written several short pieces for radio and newspapers but this is not enough.

Once more then into the breach.

Your classic mixed grill, the constituents of which I will disclose shortly, rose to ultimate prominence in this country towards the end of World War Two. On the same day that the Americans landed in Okinawa another American who happened to be a relation of my mother's landed in Ireland. His first act, after landing, was to make a beeline for the nearest hotel where he ordered a meal for himself and the members of the reception committee. He also allowed the latter to pay their individual parts of the bill, having first graciously declined to accept it himself. My mother was obliged to foot his part of it. It was not a notable occasion. There was no sparkle to the conversation. How could there be with a question-mark hanging over the matter of the bill. There was no wine. In those days wine was offered only at wakes, weddings and christenings. Ordinary people like ourselves required nothing with our meals except pepper, salt and mustard.

I remember to have ordered a mixed grill on the occasion. It is a repast which I remember with affection and respect. What's that Wordsworth said:

> The music in my heart I bore
> Long after it was heard no more.

It consisted of one medium-sized wether chop, two sizeable sausages, four slices of pudding, two black and two white, one back rasher and one streaky, a sheep's kidney, a slice of pig's liver and a large portion of potato chips which were something of a novelty at the time and were, indeed, quite foreign to many parts of the countryside. Accompanying this vast versification of varied victuals was a decent mound of steeped green peas, a large pot of tea and all the bread and butter one could wish for. It was a meal fit for a ploughman and I can proudly recount that not a vestige of any individual item remained on my plate at the close barring the chop bones alone. The total cost of this extraordinary accumulation of edibles was three shillings and sixpence which was the precise amount I had in my pocket. In those days not like now, young gentlemen would know to the nearest halfpenny the exact amount of cash on their persons. Tipping in those days, for a chap of my age, was unthinkeable.

Since that unforgettable occasion I have demolished more than my share of mixed grills. They were an ideal choice for those who were not prepared to gamble everything on a meal which consisted solely of cold meat or steak or indeed chops be they pork or mutton. If the steak or the chops were tough all was lost whereas in the mixed grill, one could find immediate redress in any of the other constituents individually or collectively.

The mixed grill was, of course, an ideal plate for peckish persons. While none of the ingredients on their own could be described as a substantial course they nevertheless succeeded in substantiating each other. If, for instance, the white pudding was not of the required consistency or if the black was too lardy one could ignore both and still make do with the other members of the confederacy.

The mixed grills greatest single attribute was its variety. All of the ingredients I have mentioned have individual characteristics which set them apart but none is capable of really standing on its own. It is the unification of all the members which gives the mixed grill its strength and intensity not to mention vivacity and colour. Some readers may carp at the fact that I have deliberately not included eggs in the association and in all fairity I should say that authorities are divided as to whether fried eggs should be included or not. I would probably agree that they should but only on condition that a major ingredient such as the liver or the kidney was absent. Traditionally, therefore, all things being in order, your fried egg is purely optional and by virtue of long association has a closer affinity to rashers.

Some of my readers will now be surprised to learn that I have not eaten a mixed grill in over a year. Strange behaviour for a man who has been so generous in his praise of mixed grills. Perhaps, however, not so strange when recent events are taken into account. Early last summer I was on my way home from the capital when I decided to stop at a wayside watering place for a pint of ale. As I sat minding my own business contemplating my dimishing measure my nostrils were assailed by a most appetising smell. I quickly finished my pint and headed for the dining-room where I was presented with a menu. There was such a diversity of foods on offer that I could not make up my mind. I, therefore, ordered a mixed grill. Here is what I got: One apology for a rack chop, two shrivelled sausages, a small wrinkled rasher and an egg more raw than fried. Finally to add to the parody, a writhing mass of badly burned onions. There was also the half of a tomato and two leaves of lettuce which I refuse to take into account. Having no wish to offend the waitress who seemed a decent sort of girl I bolted as much as I could of the mess, paid my bill and said goodbye. I should, of course, have referred the whole business over to Bord Failte but I am a tolerant man and decided to refrain from complaining. Maybe the chef had an off-day or a tiff with his wife before starting for work that morning. Who knows what choice error from the vast gallery of human misery attached itself to the poor fellow on that forgettable day.

I haven't eaten a mixed grill since. I have often felt like one but I'm afraid that I will be deceived or disappointed and so I have decided to wait for better times when people will take pride in their work once again and the mixed grill will once more titillate and tantalise those who appreciate its wonders and its subtleties.

More Books by John B. Keane

LETTERS OF A SUCCESSFUL T.D.
John B. Keane

This bestseller takes a humourous peep at the correspondence of an Irish parliamentary deputy.

LETTERS OF AN IRISH PARISH PRIEST
John B. Keane

There is a riot of laughter in every page and its theme is the correspondence between a country parish priest and his nephew who is studying to be a priest.

LETTERS OF AN IRISH PUBLICAN
John B. Keane

One of Ireland's most popular humorous authors shows us the life of a small Irish town as seen through the eyes of the local publican.

THE GENTLE ART OF MATCHMAKING and other important things
John B. Keane

An amusing collection of short essays by Ireland's most prolific writer and playwright.

LETTERS OF A LOVE-HUNGRY FARMER
John B. Keane

John B. Keane has introduced a new word into the English language — *chastitute*. This is the story of a chastitute, i.e. a man who has never lain down with a woman for reasons which are fully disclosed within this book. It is the tale of a lonely man who will not humble himself to achieve his heart's desire, whose need for female companionship whines and whimpers throughout. Here are the hilarious sex escapades of John Bosco McLane culminating finally in one dreadful deed.

LETTERS OF A COUNTRY POSTMAN
John B. Keane

A hilarious account of the exploits of a postman in rural Ireland.

LETTERS OF A MATCHMAKER
John B. Keane

Comparisons may be odious but the readers will find it fascinating to contrast the Irish matchmaking system with that of the 'Cumangettum Love Parlour' in Philadelphia. They will meet many unique characters from the Judas Jennies of New York to Fionnuala Crust of Coomasahara who buried two giant-sized, sexless husbands but eventually found happiness with a pint-sized jockey from north Cork.

LETTERS OF A CIVIC GUARD
John B. Keane

Garda Leo Molair's role is one which has been created by follies and weaknesses of his fellows. Consequently folly and weakness dominate the greater part of the correspondence of this book.

IS THE HOLY GHOST REALLY A KERRYMAN?
(And other topics of interest)
John B. Keane

Is the Holy Ghost really a Kerryman? The obvious answer to that is: if he is not a Kerryman what is he? Is he just another ghost, a mere figment of the imagination like Hamlet's father, or is he something more sinister: a Corkman masquerading as a Kerryman or worse still a real Kerryman but having an inferiority complex; that is to say a Kerryman who thinks he's only the same as everybody else?

STRONG TEA
John B. Keane

A selection of pin-pointing articles and stories from the pen of John B. Keane. Tickling the traits of our neighbours, John B. sees in the everyday actions of those around us a wealth of humour and wisdom.

SELF PORTRAIT
John B. Keane

John B. Keane's own story has all the humour and insight one would expect, but it has too the feelings of an Irish countryman for his traditional way of life and his ideas for the Ireland he loves.